The Wisdom of Jerry Garcia

The quotations in this book were excerpted from interviews with Jerry Garcia.
Published with the permission of Carol Publishing Group.

Wolf Valley Books

Distributed by The Talman Company
131 Spring Street, Suite 201E-N
New York, NY 10012

Manufactured in the United States of America
ISBN 1-888149-00-0
10 9 8 7 6 5 4 3 2 1

The Wisdom of Jerry Garcia

Wolf Valley Books
New York

I'd rather be playing.

Each organism and its consciousness has things
exactly the way it wants them all the time.

Every mind is at least as heavy as mine is.

I think of myself as a one-dimensional artist,
if I think of myself as an artist at all,
which I rarely do.

Being in the Grateful Dead
is in no way a privilege.

It's not as though we're a business trying to be a loose business; what we really are is like artists trying to survive in that half world of entertainment, which is much more conscious of its entertainment self that it is of its artist self.

Everybody's weird, everybody's bent in the Grateful Dead.

About going on stage:
I really want it to be great, and I'm terribly
disappointed if it's not.

The Grateful Dead just kind of grew out
sideways, out of the side of this social scene.

Music is like echoing, and talking about,
physical laws—at least logically, physical laws
on this planet.

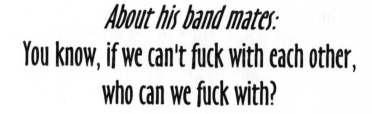

About his band mates:
You know, if we can't fuck with each other,
who can we fuck with?

It takes a long time to get interested
and to like people.

I can't believe my point of view is the only correct one.

Let's have faith in this form that has no form.
Let's have faith in this structure
that has no structure.

About the Grateful Dead:
As long as life goes on, as long as there's energy,
this thing might always want to express
itself—and need to.

The way our relationships are in the band is that we can see each other clearly and we can't see ourselves.

Reality is our own invention, which we have total access to in the most creative, direct, one-to-one sense.

About the Grateful Dead's success:
If we can do it, any-fuckin'-body can do it.

To me, it's totally amazing that we even have an audience.

I've opted for fun in this lifetime.

You never know who's going to bring you a message.

About musicians:
I've been influenced by people, too, where I haven't been influenced by the notes they played but by the attitude, the gesture--the other part of it. The substance rather than the form.

The Grateful Dead can be very powerful and people can get sucked into it in a way that can be harmful to them.

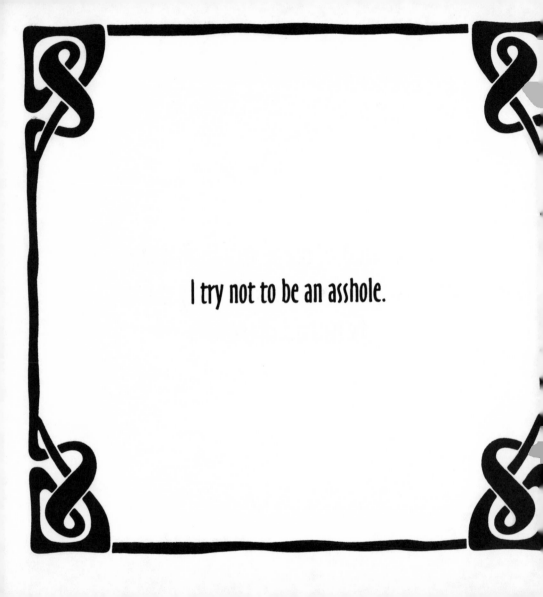

I try not to be an asshole.

People who use formula things on the audience are basically manipulating them in the same sense that fascism manipulates people.

Rhythmically, our policy is that the "one" is where you think it is. It's kind of a Zen concept, but it works well for us.

About Bob Weir:
There are always going to be things that create friction. It's part of what's interesting between he and I.

For me, it was interesting to see how other people deal with the Grateful Dead.

I try to be who I am and do what I do, you know what I mean?

If this situation says, "be outrageous," be as outrageous as you can possibly be.

I think consciousness has a place in the cosmic game, the atoms-and-universes game, the big game. I can't imagine that it's mindless—there's too much organization, and the organization is too incredible.

The Grateful Dead is truly a twenty-four-hours-
a-day thing. It doesn't ever stop.

The goal, as far as I'm concerned,
is for it to be fun.

I don't feel compromises are made on
Grateful Dead albums.

It's not enough to be good at your instrument--
you also have to be able to get
along with other musicians.

Let's go for it, because what else do we have?

About writing songs:
Every once in a while one pops out, all of a sudden it's there.

I think consciousness is really far-out stuff.

The word religion has a whole
lot of...negative to it.

We're [the band] all ambivalent about the Grateful Dead, it gets to be a love-hate thing after a while.

If you're able to enjoy something, to devote
your life to it or a reasonable amount of time
and energy, it will work out for you.

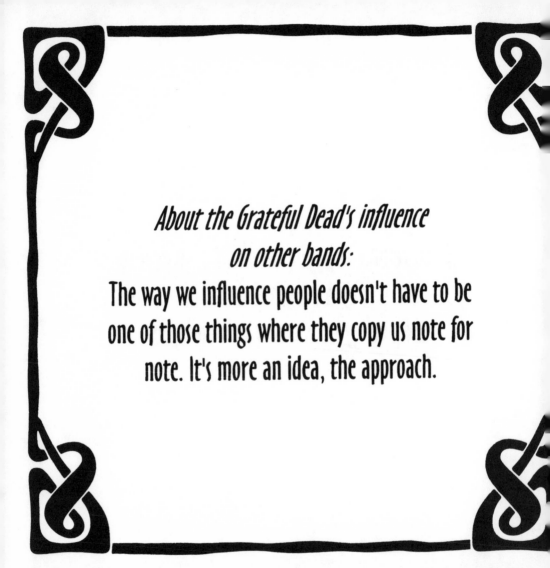

*About the Grateful Dead's influence
on other bands:*
The way we influence people doesn't have to be
one of those things where they copy us note for
note. It's more an idea, the approach.

The Grateful Dead has this weird quality, and everybody feels this.

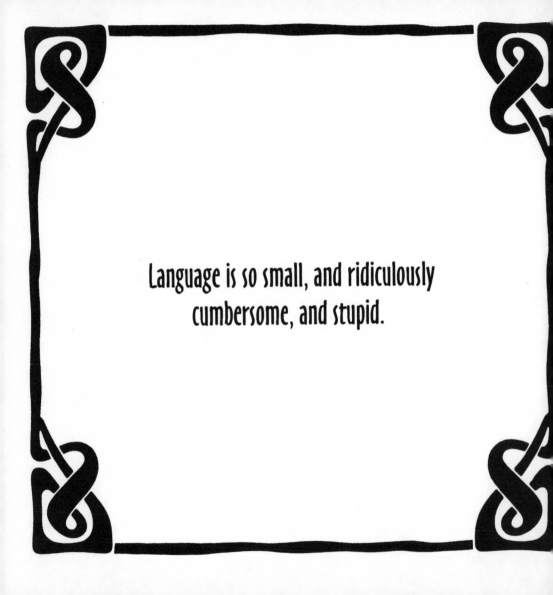

Language is so small, and ridiculously cumbersome, and stupid.

It's important to not take any bullshit, to either go whole hog or not go at all.

I've had whole other universes
dissolve and disappear.

About the Grateful Dead:
I don't know why it works.
I just know that it does.

About Bob Weir:
He's an interesting player to play with.....a lot of
our playing together that ends up having a
complementary quality to it, because we're
both so different from each other. It's neat--it
makes it fun.

Do what you have to do to not worry.

About Deadheads:
If I'm polite to them, they're usually kind and polite to me. They're good people.

That's the curse of being a musician. You can't turn your back on that part of yourself.

The way the Grateful Dead works is kind of nonlinear. Any kind of effort in a creative sense yields results on all different levels. That's the payoff of having been together for a long time: it gets you oiled.

I don't think there's a good excuse
for being unhappy.

I'd rather believe that the tendency in
consciousness is to seek freedom,
in a completely individual way.

About the Grateful Dead:
That's what fascinating; the synchronicity, how
we all arrived by these weird circuitous routes.
None of us ever planned to get to this place.

What I wonder is why...people are so afraid of everybody coming up with their own reality on their own terms.

About the Grateful Dead:
That's our strong point, if there is one: our intuitive sense.

If I had a choice who to do things with I'd rather do things with friends.

Some people really go to pieces on the road.

There's a little adventure involved in staying up
all night behind the wheel of
an eighteen-wheeler.

I know what pain is.

Perceptually, an idea that's been very important to me in playing has been the whole "odyssey" idea—journeys, voyages, you know? And adventures along the way. That whole idea has been really important to me.

What I'm after is a real great
musical experience.

I'm starting to learn how to sing.

What we're trying to do is expand
rather than narrow.

Being in the Grateful Dead is taxing in a way nothing else is. When it's hard, it's the hardest thing there is, and when it's easy, it's magic.

On playing Madison Square Garden:
I don't know whether it's the energy of the New York crowd, or whether it's just the place itself, but for some reason we play really well in there and we enjoy playing there.

About playing with the Grateful Dead:
It's definitely, truly, and authentically, a new
experience every time, and that's not bullshit.

Your best strength comes from having a secure knowledge about what's going on, having a real solid foundation and knowing where you are.

Sometimes a strange person in the crowd, a stranger would appear and say a sentence to me, and that sentence would say everything that I need to hear at that moment. It was like God speaking to you.

My mom always encouraged me—she was into music.

My mom came to one show.....That was incredible.

Perceptions are always individualized.

That's the thing about the Grateful Dead: there's this amazing richness of stuff. It just takes a long time to get it to where everybody knows all of it. A lot of it is complicated, and it requires time. Nothing else will do but time.

We were looking for good times, really, but extra-special good times with a capital G.T. Our kind of good times: good and weird.

I indulge myself.

Don't worry—be happy! That's it! That's the best thing I've ever heard.

I'm only human.

You can't play the way the Grateful Dead plays
without working at it.

We want the Grateful Dead to be something
that isn't the result of tricks.

Music stores are full of guys that play real great but don't have either the ability to get along with other musicians or don't have a personal statement to make personally.

Notes for me have shape
and form and...color.

It's really difficult to extrapolate from the Grateful Dead to the music business or the music scene....We're like the exception to every rule. We're in some kind of nonformula, nonlinear developmental path.

On Playing on the West Coast and East Coast:
We play with Great sensitivity and clarity here
[in California]....We play with greater
energy there.

It's been truly fantastic.

I keep saying it's like we're just getting started.

About the appeal of the Grateful Dead:
There's no way that any amount of telling of it
is ever going to reveal it to the point of
demystifying it. It's much too complex.

You get your ups and your downs. I've always assumed that something like the laws of karma prevail. Something good happens, something bad's going to happen of equal volume.

Turn your friends on.

You've got to be light on your feet.

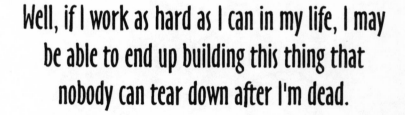

Well, if I work as hard as I can in my life, I may
be able to end up building this thing that
nobody can tear down after I'm dead.